THE SOUNDLESS SOUND

TEACHINGS OF
THE ORDER OF CHRISTIAN MYSTICS

THE SOUNDLESS
SOUND

TEACHINGS OF THE ORDER OF CHRISTIAN MYSTICS
THE "CURTISS BOOKS" FREELY AVAILABLE AT
WWW.ORDEROFCHRISTIANMYSTICS.CO.ZA

1. THE VOICE OF ISIS
2. THE MESSAGE OF AQUARIA
3. THE INNER RADIANCE
4. REALMS OF THE LIVING DEAD
5. COMING WORLD CHANGES
6. THE KEY TO THE UNIVERSE
7. THE KEY OF DESTINY
8. LETTERS FROM THE TEACHER VOLUME I
9. LETTERS FROM THE TEACHER VOLUME II
10. THE TRUTH ABOUT EVOLUTION AND THE BIBLE
11. THE PHILOSOPHY OF WAR
12. PERSONAL SURVIVAL
13. THE PATTERN LIFE
14. FOUR-FOLD HEALTH
15. VITAMINS
16. WHY ARE WE HERE?
17. REINCARNATION
18. FOR YOUNG SOULS
19. GEMS OF MYSTICISM
20. THE TEMPLE OF SILENCE
21. THE DIVINE MOTHER
22. THE SOUNDLESS SOUND
23. THE MYSTIC LIFE
24. THE LOVE OF RABIACCA
25. POTENT PRAYERS
SUPPORTING VOLUMES
26. THE SEVENTH SEAL
27. TOWARDS THE LIGHT

THE SOUNDLESS SOUND

By
THE TEACHER
of
𝕿𝖍𝖊 𝕺𝖗𝖉𝖊𝖗 𝖔𝖋 𝖙𝖍𝖊 15

Transcribed by
HARRIETTE AUGUSTA CURTISS
and
F. HOMER CURTISS, B.S., M.D.
Founders of
THE ORDER OF CHRISTIAN MYSTICS
and
AUTHORS OF THE "CURTISS BOOKS"

2012 EDITION

REPUBLISHED FOR THE ORDER BY
MOUNT LINDEN PUBLISHING
JOHANNESBURG, SOUTH AFRICA
ISBN: 978-1-920483-10-4

"Ministers of Christ and Stewards of the Mysteries of God."
1 Corinthians 4 vs. 1

DEDICATION

THE VOICE has spoken.

To those who can hear and in whose hearts an echo of the Soundless Sound has thrilled, this little booklet is dedicated.

"Out of the silence that is peace a resonant voice shall arise. . . . Listen to the song of life. Store in your memory the melody you hear. Learn from it the lesson of harmony."

Light on the Path, ii.

"God thundereth marvellously with His voice; great things doeth He, which we cannot comprehend."

Job xxxvii:5.

FOREWORD

THIS little book comes to you, dear reader, as a messenger winged with the love of the Master Who would gather His children from the four winds.

¶ To all who are yearning for love and understanding, who are weary of waiting for the eventide when the master shall walk in His garden in the cool of the day to meet His disciples, this little booklet is sent.

¶ It comes as a cooling breeze at twilight after the heat and toil of the day. It comes as the song of birds piping their goodnight to the toil-worn. It comes as a messenger of Peace, speaking to such hearts as can hear, bringing to them the assurance that in the midst of the toil and disappointments and weariness of life there is a surging undercurrent of Power and Peace sweeping all humanity onward and upward, drawing them closer to the Heart of Love.

¶ This little book is but a tiny rill from the Fountain of Life. If it but fill with cooling drops the cup of one weary wanderer fainting in the Desert of Life, it has fulfilled its mission.

¶ It is cast upon the Waters of Life in Love, Compassion and Truth, knowing that it will accomplish that for which it is sent forth.

THE SOUNDLESS SOUND

O YE seekers for the Way! Ye whose ears are yet deaf to the Soundless Sound!

¶ To you comes a message from all the spheres through which the Spirit of Life Eternal presses onward, pulsating, rising, falling, beating the outward form into nothingness that the immortal Spirit of all things may be revealed to you, the Soundless Sound.

¶ Why hear ye not?

¶ Ye are so eagerly listening to the sounds that are without, to the babel of outer happenings, to the babel of your thoughts.

¶ Man's thoughts are the world's babel in miniature.

¶ That which should be a deep flowing river of consciousness is but the babble of a shallow brook. Ye are wont to babble mentally, to hold mental conversations about the trivial occurrences that have impinged upon your consciousness from the outer manifestations of life. As the constant drip of water wears away the solid rock, so this wasted force exhausts the brain and stultifies the spiritual consciousness as would continued chatter of trifling things.

¶ Alas, how oft these mental conversations are of matters unmentionable in outward speech!

K NOW ye not that aimless mental activity forms a shell about you shutting you away from the Voice of God which should speak in your heart?

¶ The first lesson for ye who seek to consciously enter The Path is to control the currents of your thoughts.[1]

¶ Until the mind is controlled and entertains only that which you desire you still live in the world of sensation, still seek the True within the false, the living among the dead.

¶ Know ye not that all outward seem-

---

[1] See Lesson on *The Path*.

═══════════════════════════════

ing, altho but an illusion born of the senses, is nevertheless a covering or veil that hides the True? a dark-lantern within which the Shekina glows?

L OOK throughout Nature. You find not one perfect or complete creation. Not one blossom is without defect, one tree without its dropping leaves and dying branches, its gnarled and crooked trunk or other imperfections. Not one blade of grass but has some flaw, is eaten by some insect or dies for want of moisture.

¶ Nothing in all Nature is perfect.

¶ Yet stand upon the mountain-top and view the scene outspread before you. The landscape has many minor defects if examined closely. Not one form is perfect or complete, yet as a whole they present a picture that is grand, inspiring. How your heart thrills with joy unspeakable!

¶ "How wondrous! Behold the handiwork of God."

¶ You know the thorns are there, yet the rose breathes love and joy.

¶ What in this imperfect world of Nature speaks so distinctly, so persistently to your heart? It is

THE SOUNDLESS SOUND

that Divine Power which lies veiled behind all the imperfections.

L OOK into the hearts of men, into the hearts of your chosen companions. There again you will find many, many defects.

¶ Who has found a perfect human being?

¶ Who has found one personality in whom all ideals are fulfilled? No more than you have found one leaf without blemish in all Nature.

¶ Why can ye not look upon humanity and feel the same warm thrill of love ye feel for imperfect Nature? Why criticize and condemn your fellowman more than the herbs of the field?

❡ Through man's free will he has created and is responsible for all Nature's imperfections. A Divine Ideal deflected by the prism of man's misconception. A literal working out of the prophesy: "Cursed is the ground for thy sake; thorns also and thistles shall it bring forth to thee."[2]

❡ It is this law, altho unrecognized, which makes you condemn your fellowman, overlooking your own share in creating these conditions.

❡ You listen not to the silent Voice of God, the Voice of the Silence, hence do not recognize your own creations. You close your ears to the Soundless Sound that is speaking through all Nature, and within the hearts of all your fellow pilgrims; that is singing

[2] *Genesis, iii.*

within the hearts of your friends, yea, and your enemies also.

℘ Just as the ineffable charm of a landscape appeals to you in spite of its defects, so should you recognize the Soundless Sound speaking through you in no uncertain language, even though imperfections be apparent.

℘ Meditate upon this thought in your dealings with your fellowmen.

℘ Many, with all their hearts, believe there is a Divine Power manifesting through humanity, yet, alas, how few there be who seek or recognize it!

MANY believe that by much experience, much prayer, arduous struggle and patient endurance, one day they may hear the Voice speak to their hearts, pointing out their next step in evolution; perhaps speaking in admonition; perhaps saying: "Well done, good and faithful servant, enter thou into the joy of thy Lord."

¶ How few realize that the voice of humanity is in reality the Voice of God, but in quite a different sense from the usual interpretation of "Vox populi, vox Deus!"

¶ Through every heart, in spite of its defects and failings, back of the personality which may be obnoxious, beneath and beyond is the Voice of God speaking. And this Voice is the one Voice in all, making humanity one.

¶ "Call it by what name you will, it is a voice that speaks where there is none to speak—it is a messenger that comes, a messenger without form or substance; or it is the flower of the soul that has opened."[3]

¶ It speaks to you from the lips of the prattling babe, from the eyes of the weary toiler or from the mouth of the reckless, the profligate or the fallen sister. Back of <u>every</u> manifestation of life on this plane of being stands Divinity.

¶ Until you have learned this lesson you cannot pass on.

¶ Until you recognize Divinity speaking to you from every other atom of humanity;

¶ Until you have ceased to seek out your brother's mistakes; until you have ceased to look for his shortcomings and failings; ceased to measure his corn by your bushel of human

---

[3] *Light on The Path*, Part 1.

frailty and have found how to use God's measure instead;

¶ Until you have ceased to listen to the many voices of the world and begun to listen to the one Divine Voice manifesting through all humanity as through Nature, you will never hear the Silent Voice within.

AMID the rolling fields and wooded hills, while listening to the symphony of Nature sounds—the song of bird, the drone of insects, the rustle of leafy bough, the tinkle of brook or boom of sea—you are uplifted and stirred by a sense of The Divine surrounding you and coming close. You have caught a glimpse of Divine Consciousness. Your Soul responds to the Soundless Sound.

❡ When your Soul thrills with the same oneness as you contact your fellowmen you will then have ceased, at least in a measure, to listen to the many and hearken to the One.

❡ Then are you ready to come into Truth; to find Truth and understand that it is the foundation of all things; that underneath and within the innermost sanctuary of all manifestations of life is Divine Love.

❡ Then will you know that this is not a world of confusion, of strange and mysterious happenings, but a world of Law and Love, a world of manifold expressions of Deity. Then and then only are you ready to listen to the Voice which speaks to you in the Silence, the Soundless Sound.

¶ Then you will realize that you need not desert the haunts of men, live in the wilderness, mortify the flesh, live on roots and herbs, quench your thirst at the mountain streamlet. Your opportunity will confront you wherever you are placed. You will find great joy ministering to each atom of humanity you meet. You will have found the One in all. Then will the Voice become the daily Friend, the everlasting Counselor, the Prince of Peace, the God of Love within your heart.

TO HEAR this Voice no psychic or occult powers are needed, altho in time it will manifest in a definite way on the psychic and mental planes.

¶ This Voice you so eagerly desire must first be heard and recognized in all things ere it can be condensed and manifest consciously in your heart, for

¶ This animating principle of Divinity speaks to you in no uncertain tones on every plane of Being. Make it practical.

¶ You must dwell with God ere you can think God's thoughts or respond to the vibrations of His Soundless Voice.

¶ The physical is the lowest plane of manifestation. If you are deaf to the Voice upon the physical plane and think to hear it upon the psychic or mental planes it may seem to fail you altogether.

❡ Or you will find yourself listening to astral voices which are ever ready to fulfill that which you desire. But such voices ultimately lead astray, even though expressing lofty sentiments at first and giving apparent good counsel.

KNOW ye not the conditions of life in which you find yourself are those best fitted for your Soul-growth?

❡ Be true O Soul and dare to stand in the inner sanctuary of your heart and face yourself. Know that you, too, sometimes vibrate falsely, yet within are true.

❡ Recognize this and at once you will recognize the true within each

Soul, even those who, because of vibrations
not in harmony with Truth as revealed to you,
are neither pleasing nor helpful.

¶ Learn to pass such Souls by, but without
condemnation, learning your lesson.

¶ If they express what is opposite to Truth
as seen by you, learn to express more Truth
because of their example. From them learn
to send forth stronger vibrations of Truth.
Only thus can you help them, never by
condemnation.

¶ Let each Soul vibrate to its own center, as
you vibrate to yours. In the Grand Man, as
in the human body, there are many centers.
Perfect harmony means each atom vibrating to

its own center while all respond to the One
Life.

¶ Then shall you know the Psalm of Life.
Then shall the sacred joy, the great peace that
comes to those who live with Truth, enter into
you.

INHARMONY is self-produced by your
unwillingness to let each live his own life.
Learn well this lesson.

¶ Then shall the Soundless Sound, which
echoes in each heart and makes all the world
akin, sing to you of gladness. And it will say
that only as you forget self, let the little personal self be swallowed up in the Great Self,[4]
can you become a conscious note in the great
symphony.

---

[4] See Lesson on *The Self*.

❡ Only when you find your greatest joy in bringing happiness to others, not seeking how to be happy, how to be loved, or how best to live close to the Divine for yourself alone, only then can real abiding happiness and close companionship of the Voice be yours.

❡ Then will you find that the sorrow and misery of life which so oppressed you has been swallowed up in a comprehension of the great Plan of Redemption. Give thanks for every step that has brought you to the realization that you are a conscious factor in this great work. Because of this Voice you have learned to know and love, you can enter the hearts of others, can enter into the joy of the One Life. It is not your brother or sister who brings this joy to you, but the One Voice in the Soul of all.

HEED lest having reached this step you go astray; lest in the zeal of self-sacrifice you seek to bear all burdens that others may go free.

❡ Be just first to yourself that you may be just to others.

❡ Know well the burdens of all Souls are sent in Love. Deprive them not of the strength they bring, lest, alas, for lack of the burden you would bear they should lose the prize.

❡ Discriminate between justice and selfishness.

❡ Say not in presumptious pride that

you will bear all suffering. Say rather you will uplift the world by <u>being</u> better and happier yourself.

MISERY, like happiness, is contagious. To be miserable is but to increase the misery of the world. The Psalm of Life which you seek to bear is not a wail of misery, but a pæan of joy.

¶ Through thoughtless selfishness perchance you bring sorrow to another and go your way, sharing it not. But you cannot bring one joy, even to the least of your brethren, that your own Soul is not filled with the same joy, yea, a greater joy, for the joy you feel is the joy of the One Life surging through the universe. By your own effort you have opened a door and permitted it to flow through you. You have sounded a note on the great Harp of Life and its vibrations will never cease. They shall spread from sphere to sphere and open to you the Melody of the Divine, the Soundless Sound.

¶ Therefore we are not all one in sorrow, for sorrow is not immortal and has no existence in the One Life. It belongs wholly to earth, is one of the imperfections of separated existence. It must pass away. Just as every imperfection in Nature will be transmuted as the Divine is deflected less and less by man's imperfect prism. "Sorrow may endure for a night, but joy cometh in the morning."

M ANY who have lost a dear companion feel it a melancholy duty to shut their hearts away from joy and dwell in sorrow. This, instead of pleasing the departed, keeps them from the joy awaiting them. The voice of The Christ is continually saying: "Rejoice in the Lord alway: and again I say, Rejoice."

¶ If you would hear this Voice in the conditions of earth, strive to awaken it by deeds of loving-kindness. Just the natural little kindnesses that bring joy into life. Also watch that your features take not on a doleful expression, or of superiority, pride and condescension.

¶ A joyful countenance will brighten the day for many a weary Soul.

℘ Should sorrow or misfortune overtake you turn your mind to the joy of the One Life, away from the petty worries that are barriers to its manifestation.

WHEN, little by little, you have learned to hear the Soundless Sound in the hearts of all creatures in the physical world, then will it begin to manifest in your mental world. It will take form in your heart, will cheer and comfort you.

℘ When you have listened to and obeyed the God within, the Higher Self who is one with all will make his own Voice heard.

THE mind is the slayer of the self, but the Voice is the slayer of the mind. Only Spiritual Sound can quiet the voice of the mind when it reflects the confusions of earthly thoughts. Only The Christ walking upon the troubled waters of your life can say: "Peace, be still."

¶ This is the Pentacostal Flame that rests upon your head. As it manifests all defects are consumed. It burns away the barriers of the flesh that separate you from humanity, permitting you to see the Divine in all.

¶ In the mental world the Flame burns out the thought of personality, that the Real Self may manifest.

¶ In the spiritual world the Flame becomes the All-Seeing Eye, the Shekina, the Star of Initiation, the Light which shall guide you into that peace which passeth understanding.

¶ You no longer think of this Divine One Life. You live it. You become it. You enter into the Silence and become the Voice itself!

O YE seekers who are one with all that is! Know ye not that the power is yours to awaken Divine Harmony in life?

¶ Into your hands is given the Harp of Life, whose strings give forth the seven creative notes. Strike the Strings aright! Its tones are all joy and love and oneness.

♩ Learn to play upon this Harp as you would learn to play an instrument of earth. First learn to strike one note true and clear, then chords, and finally melodies and symphonies. Your Divine Teacher is ever present.

♩ If in your heart there comes a shadow of gloom or sadness, turn away and sound a note of joy in some other heart and yours shall be filled!

♩ Look today out over the world and sound a melody of joy and gladness!

♩ Strike the chords! Listen to the Soundless Sound that sweeps with divine melody through your heart!

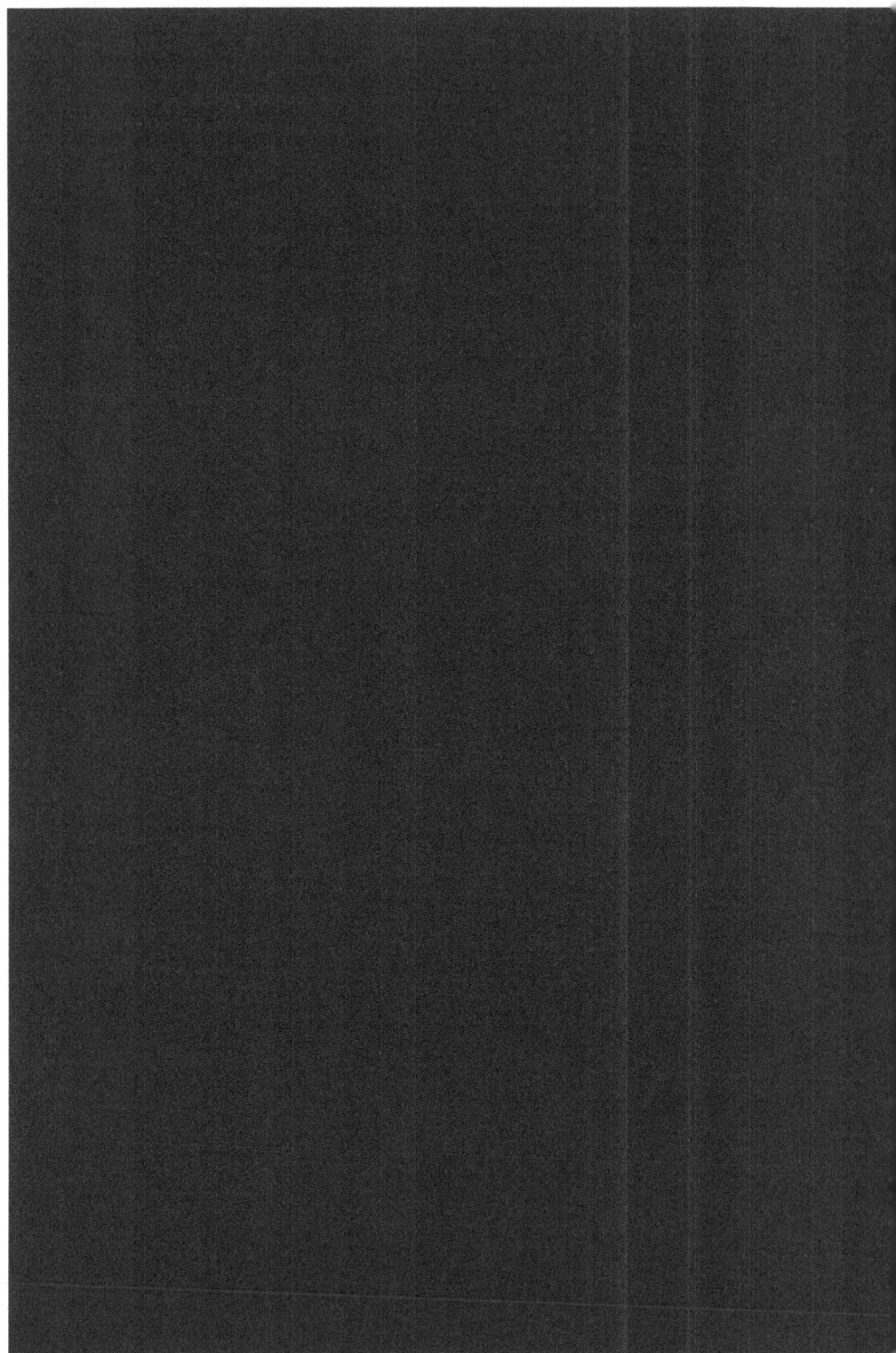

www.ingramcontent.com/pod-product-compliance
Lightning Source LLC
Chambersburg PA
CBHW071750020426
42331CB00008B/2257